CHINESE
HOROSCOPES
FOR
LOVERS

The
Horse

LORI REID

illustrated by
PAUL COLLICUTT

ELEMENT BOOKS

Shaftesbury, Dorset • Rockport, Massachusetts • Brisbane, Queensland

© Lori Reid 1996
First published in Great Britain in 1996 by
ELEMENT BOOKS LIMITED
Shaftesbury, Dorset SP7 8BP

Published in the USA in 1996 by
ELEMENT BOOKS, INC.
PO Box 830, Rockport, MA 01966

Published in Australia in 1996 by
ELEMENT BOOKS LIMITED
for JACARANDA WILEY LIMITED
33 Park Road, Milton, Brisbane 4064

Designed and created by
THE BRIDGEWATER BOOK COMPANY
Art directed by *Peter Bridgewater*
Designed by *Angela Neal*
Picture research by *Vanessa Fletcher*
Edited by *Gillian Delaforce*

Printed and bound in Great Britain by
BPC Paulton Books Ltd

British Library Cataloguing in Publication data available

Library of Congress Cataloging in Publication data available

ISBN 1-85230-767-6

Contents

THE
HORSE

馬

8

*Why are
some people
lucky in
love and
others not?*

Chinese Astrology

SOME PEOPLE fall in love and, as the fairy tales go, live happily ever after. Others fall in love – again and again, make the same mistakes every time and never form a lasting relationship. Most of us come between these two extremes,

and some people form remarkably successful unions while others make spectacular disasters of their personal lives. Why are some people lucky in love while others have the odds stacked against them?

ANIMAL NAMES
According to the philosophy of the Far East, luck has very little to do with it. The answer, the philosophers say, lies with 'the Animal that hides in our hearts'. This Animal, of which there are 12, forms part of the complex art of Chinese Astrology. Each year of a 12-year cycle is attributed an Animal sign, whose characteristics are said to influence worldly events as well as the personality and fate of each living thing that comes under its dominion. The 12 Animals run in sequence, beginning with the Rat and followed by the Ox, Tiger, Rabbit, Dragon, Snake, Horse, Sheep, Monkey, Rooster, Dog and last, but not least, the Pig. Being born in the Year of the Ox, for example, is simply a way of describing what you're like, physically and psychologically. And this is quite different from someone who, for instance, is born in the Year of the Snake.

馬
9

The 12 Animals of Chinese Astrology.

RELATIONSHIPS

These Animal names are merely the tip of the iceberg, considering the complexity of the whole subject. Yet such are the richness and wisdom of Chinese Astrology that understanding the principles behind the year in which you were born will give you powerful insights into your own personality. The system is very specific about which Animals are compatible and which are antagonistic and this tells us whether our relationships will be successful. Marriages are made in heaven, so the saying goes. The heavens, according to Chinese beliefs, can point the way. The rest is up to us.

馬

10

Year Chart and Birth Dates

UNLIKE THE WESTERN CALENDAR, which is based on the Sun, the Oriental year is based on the movement of the Moon, which means that New Year's Day does not fall on a fixed date. This Year Chart, taken from the Chinese Perpetual Calendar, lists the dates on which each year begins and ends together with its Animal ruler for the year. In addition, the Chinese believe that the tangible world is composed of 5 elements, each slightly adapting the characteristics of the Animal signs. These elemental influences are also given here. Finally, the aspect, that is, whether the year is characteristically Yin (-) or Yang (+), is also listed.

The Western calendar is based on the Sun; the Oriental on the Moon.

YIN AND YANG

Yin and Yang are the terms given to the dynamic complementary forces that keep the universe in balance and which are the central principles behind life. Yin is all that is considered negative, passive, feminine, night, the Moon, while Yang is considered positive, active, masculine, day, the Sun.

馬

11

Year	From – To	Animal sign	Element	Aspect	
1900	31 Jan 1900 – 18 Feb 1901	Rat	Metal	+	Yang
1901	19 Feb 1901 – 7 Feb 1902	Ox	Metal	–	Yin
1902	8 Feb 1902 – 28 Jan 1903	Tiger	Water	+	Yang
1903	29 Jan 1903 – 15 Feb 1904	Rabbit	Water	–	Yin
1904	16 Feb 1904 – 3 Feb 1905	Dragon	Wood	+	Yang
1905	4 Feb 1905 – 24 Jan 1906	Snake	Wood	–	Yin
1906	25 Jan 1906 – 12 Feb 1907	Horse	Fire	+	Yang
1907	13 Feb 1907 – 1 Feb 1908	Sheep	Fire	–	Yin
1908	2 Feb 1908 – 21 Jan 1909	Monkey	Earth	+	Yang
1909	22 Jan 1909 – 9 Feb 1910	Rooster	Earth	–	Yin
1910	10 Feb 1910 – 29 Jan 1911	Dog	Metal	+	Yang
1911	30 Jan 1911 – 17 Feb 1912	Pig	Metal	–	Yin
1912	18 Feb 1912 – 5 Feb 1913	Rat	Water	+	Yang
1913	6 Feb 1913 – 25 Jan 1914	Ox	Water	–	Yin
1914	26 Jan 1914 – 13 Feb 1915	Tiger	Wood	+	Yang
1915	14 Feb 1915 – 2 Feb 1916	Rabbit	Wood	–	Yin
1916	3 Feb 1916 – 22 Jan 1917	Dragon	Fire	+	Yang
1917	23 Jan 1917 – 10 Feb 1918	Snake	Fire	–	Yin
1918	11 Feb 1918 – 31 Jan 1919	Horse	Earth	+	Yang
1919	1 Feb 1919 – 19 Feb 1920	Sheep	Earth	–	Yin
1920	20 Feb 1920 – 7 Feb 1921	Monkey	Metal	+	Yang
1921	8 Feb 1921 – 27 Jan 1922	Rooster	Metal	–	Yin
1922	28 Jan 1922 – 15 Feb 1923	Dog	Water	+	Yang
1923	16 Feb 1923 – 4 Feb 1924	Pig	Water	–	Yin
1924	5 Feb 1924 – 24 Jan 1925	Rat	Wood	+	Yang
1925	25 Jan 1925 – 12 Feb 1926	Ox	Wood	–	Yin
1926	13 Feb 1926 – 1 Feb 1927	Tiger	Fire	+	Yang
1927	2 Feb 1927 – 22 Jan 1928	Rabbit	Fire	–	Yin
1928	23 Jan 1928 – 9 Feb 1929	Dragon	Earth	+	Yang
1929	10 Feb 1929 – 29 Jan 1930	Snake	Earth	–	Yin
1930	30 Jan 1930 – 16 Feb 1931	Horse	Metal	+	Yang
1931	17 Feb 1931 – 5 Feb 1932	Sheep	Metal	–	Yin
1932	6 Feb 1932 – 25 Jan 1933	Monkey	Water	+	Yang
1933	26 Jan 1933 – 13 Feb 1934	Rooster	Water	–	Yin
1934	14 Feb 1934 – 3 Feb 1935	Dog	Wood	+	Yang
1935	4 Feb 1935 – 23 Jan 1936	Pig	Wood	–	Yin

馬

12

Year	From – To		Animal sign	Element	Aspect	
1936	24 Jan 1936 – 10 Feb 1937		Rat	Fire	+	Yang
1937	11 Feb 1937 – 30 Jan 1938		Ox	Fire	−	Yin
1938	31 Jan 1938 – 18 Feb 1939		Tiger	Earth	+	Yang
1939	19 Feb 1939 – 7 Feb 1940		Rabbit	Earth	−	Yin
1940	8 Feb 1940 – 26 Jan 1941		Dragon	Metal	+	Yang
1941	27 Jan 1941 – 14 Feb 1942		Snake	Metal	−	Yin
1942	15 Feb 1942 – 4 Feb 1943		Horse	Water	+	Yang
1943	5 Feb 1943 – 24 Jan 1944		Sheep	Water	−	Yin
1944	25 Jan 1944 – 12 Feb 1945		Monkey	Wood	+	Yang
1945	13 Feb 1945 – 1 Feb 1946		Rooster	Wood	−	Yin
1946	2 Feb 1946 – 21 Jan 1947		Dog	Fire	+	Yang
1947	22 Jan 1947 – 9 Feb 1948		Pig	Fire	−	Yin
1948	10 Feb 1948 – 28 Jan 1949		Rat	Earth	+	Yang
1949	29 Jan 1949 – 16 Feb 1950		Ox	Earth	−	Yin
1950	17 Feb 1950 – 5 Feb 1951		Tiger	Metal	+	Yang
1951	6 Feb 1951 – 26 Jan 1952		Rabbit	Metal	−	Yin
1952	27 Jan 1952 – 13 Feb 1953		Dragon	Water	+	Yang
1953	14 Feb 1953 – 2 Feb 1954		Snake	Water	−	Yin
1954	3 Feb 1954 – 23 Jan 1955		Horse	Wood	+	Yang
1955	24 Jan 1955 – 11 Feb 1956		Sheep	Wood	−	Yin
1956	12 Feb 1956 – 30 Jan 1957		Monkey	Fire	+	Yang
1957	31 Jan 1957 – 17 Feb 1958		Rooster	Fire	−	Yin
1958	18 Feb 1958 – 7 Feb 1959		Dog	Earth	+	Yang
1959	8 Feb 1959 – 27 Jan 1960		Pig	Earth	−	Yin
1960	28 Jan 1960 – 14 Feb 1961		Rat	Metal	+	Yang
1961	15 Feb 1961 – 4 Feb 1962		Ox	Metal	−	Yin
1962	5 Feb 1962 – 24 Jan 1963		Tiger	Water	+	Yang
1963	25 Jan 1963 – 12 Feb 1964		Rabbit	Water	−	Yin
1964	13 Feb 1964 – 1 Feb 1965		Dragon	Wood	+	Yang
1965	2 Feb 1965 – 20 Jan 1966		Snake	Wood	−	Yin
1966	21 Jan 1966 – 8 Feb 1967		Horse	Fire	+	Yang
1967	9 Feb 1967 – 29 Jan 1968		Sheep	Fire	−	Yin
1968	30 Jan 1968 – 16 Feb 1969		Monkey	Earth	+	Yang
1969	17 Feb 1969 – 5 Feb 1970		Rooster	Earth	−	Yin
1970	6 Feb 1970 – 26 Jan 1971		Dog	Metal	+	Yang
1971	27 Jan 1971 – 15 Jan 1972		Pig	Metal	−	Yin

馬

13

Year	From – To		Animal sign	Element	Aspect	
1972	16 Jan 1972 – 2 Feb 1973		Rat	Water	+	Yang
1973	3 Feb 1973 – 22 Jan 1974		Ox	Water	–	Yin
1974	23 Jan 1974 – 10 Feb 1975		Tiger	Wood	+	Yang
1975	11 Feb 1975 – 30 Jan 1976		Rabbit	Wood	–	Yin
1976	31 Jan 1976 – 17 Feb 1977		Dragon	Fire	+	Yang
1977	18 Feb 1977 – 6 Feb 1978		Snake	Fire	–	Yin
1978	7 Feb 1978 – 27 Jan 1979		Horse	Earth	+	Yang
1979	28 Jan 1979 – 15 Feb 1980		Sheep	Earth	–	Yin
1980	16 Feb 1980 – 4 Feb 1981		Monkey	Metal	+	Yang
1981	5 Feb 1981 – 24 Jan 1982		Rooster	Metal	–	Yin
1982	25 Jan 1982 – 12 Feb 1983		Dog	Water	+	Yang
1983	13 Feb 1983 – 1 Feb 1984		Pig	Water	–	Yin
1984	2 Feb 1984 – 19 Feb 1985		Rat	Wood	+	Yang
1985	20 Feb 1985 – 8 Feb 1986		Ox	Wood	–	Yin
1986	9 Feb 1986 – 28 Jan 1987		Tiger	Fire	+	Yang
1987	29 Jan 1987 – 16 Feb 1988		Rabbit	Fire	–	Yin
1988	17 Feb 1988 – 5 Feb 1989		Dragon	Earth	+	Yang
1989	6 Feb 1989 – 26 Jan 1990		Snake	Earth	–	Yin
1990	27 Jan 1990 – 14 Feb 1991		Horse	Metal	+	Yang
1991	15 Feb 1991 – 3 Feb 1992		Sheep	Metal	–	Yin
1992	4 Feb 1992 – 22 Jan 1993		Monkey	Water	+	Yang
1993	23 Jan 1993 – 9 Feb 1994		Rooster	Water	–	Yin
1994	10 Feb 1994 – 30 Jan 1995		Dog	Wood	+	Yang
1995	31 Jan 1995 – 18 Feb 1996		Pig	Wood	–	Yin
1996	19 Feb 1996 – 7 Feb 1997		Rat	Fire	+	Yang
1997	8 Feb 1997 – 27 Jan 1998		Ox	Fire	–	Yin
1998	28 Jan 1998 – 15 Feb 1999		Tiger	Earth	+	Yang
1999	16 Feb 1999 – 4 Feb 2000		Rabbit	Earth	–	Yin
2000	5 Feb 2000 – 23 Jan 2001		Dragon	Metal	+	Yang
2001	24 Jan 2001 – 11 Feb 2002		Snake	Metal	–	Yin
2002	12 Feb 2002 – 31 Jan 2003		Horse	Water	+	Yang
2003	1 Feb 2003 – 21 Jan 2004		Sheep	Water	–	Yin
2004	22 Jan 2004 – 8 Feb 2005		Monkey	Wood	+	Yang
2005	9 Feb 2005 – 28 Jan 2006		Rooster	Wood	–	Yin
2006	29 Jan 2006 – 17 Feb 2007		Dog	Fire	+	Yang
2007	18 Feb 2007 – 6 Feb 2008		Pig	Fire	–	Yin

THE
HORSE

馬

14

Introducing the Animals

THE RAT ♥ ♥ ♥ DRAGON, MONKEY ✖ HORSE

Outwardly cool, Rats are passionate lovers with depths of feeling that others don't often recognize. Rats are very self-controlled.

THE OX ♥ ♥ ♥ SNAKE, ROOSTER ✖ SHEEP

Not necessarily the most romantic of the signs, Ox people make steadfast lovers as well as faithful, affectionate partners.

THE TIGER ♥ ♥ ♥ HORSE, DOG ✖ MONKEY

Passionate and sensual, Tigers are exciting lovers. Flirty when young, once committed they make stable partners and keep their sexual allure.

THE RABBIT ♥ ♥ ♥ SHEEP, PIG ✖ ROOSTER

Gentle, emotional and sentimental, Rabbits make sensitive lovers. They are shrewd and seek a partner who offers security.

THE DRAGON ♥ ♥ ♥ RAT, MONKEY ✖ DOG

Dragon folk get as much stimulation from mind-touch as they do through sex. A partner on the same wave-length is essential.

THE SNAKE ♥ ♥ ♥ OX, ROOSTER ✖ PIG

Deeply passionate, strongly sexed but not aggressive, snakes are attracted to elegant, refined partners. But they are deeply jealous and possessive.

♥ ♥ ♥ *COMPATIBLE*   ✖ *INCOMPATIBLE*

| THE HORSE | ♥ ♥ ♥ TIGER, DOG | ✖ RAT |

For horse-born folk love is blind. In losing their hearts, they lose their heads and make several mistakes before finding the right partner.

| THE SHEEP | ♥ ♥ ♥ RABBIT, PIG | ✖ OX |

Sheep-born people are made for marriage. Domesticated home-lovers, they find emotional satisfaction with a partner who provides security.

| THE MONKEY | ♥ ♥ ♥ DRAGON, RAT | ✖ TIGER |

Clever and witty, Monkeys need partners who will keep them stimulated. Forget the 9 to 5 routine, these people need *pizzazz*.

| THE ROOSTER | ♥ ♥ ♥ OX, SNAKE | ✖ RABBIT |

The Rooster's stylish good looks guarantee they will attract many suitors. They are level-headed and approach relationships coolly.

| THE DOG | ♥ ♥ ♥ TIGER, HORSE | ✖ DRAGON |

A loving, stable relationship is an essential component in the lives of Dogs. Once they have found their mate, they remain faithful for life.

| THE PIG | ♥ ♥ ♥ RABBIT, SHEEP | ✖ SNAKE |

These are sensual hedonists who enjoy lingering love-making between satin sheets. Caviar and champagne go down very nicely too.

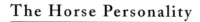

The Horse Personality

AS A MEMBER OF THE HORSE CLAN, you're a bright social star. Bursting with life, vivacity and irrepressible enthusiasm, you explode onto the scene, the effortless life and soul of the party, amusing all and sundry with your sparkling wit and lively repartee and then, kicking up your heels and accelerating in seconds from a standing start to a furious gallop, you head off to the next pasture that takes your fancy.

HORSE FACTS

Seventh in order ★ *Chinese name – Ma*
★ *Sign of elegance and fervour* ★ *Hour – 11AM–12.59PM* ★
★ *Month – June* ★ *Western counterpart – Gemini* ★

CHARACTERISTICS

♥ *Vivacity* ♥ *Stamina* ♥ *Wit* ♥ *Independence*
♥ *Cheerfulness* ♥ *Refinement* ♥ *Friendliness*

✖ *Selfishness* ✖ *Volatility* ✖ *Impatience*
✖ *Inconstancy* ✖ *Vanity* ✖ *Recklessness*

A MASTER JUGGLER

That you're impulsive and highly volatile is indisputable. That you're also erratic and whimsical, no-one could deny; yet you're intelligent and practical too. You're bright as a button with a mind that's razor-sharp, able to pick up new skills in the twinkling of an eye. And you're a master juggler too, adept at carrying on several conversations at once or at holding down two or three jobs at the same time. You can keep disparate projects in the air while attending to whatever is currently on hand.

馬

17

Horse people love to prance in the eye of a hurricane of activity.

HORSE ENERGY

As a Horse you love to live life at a headlong gallop. Wherever you go you carry a vortex of high-octane activity around with you. Inexhaustible and indefatigable are terms often used to describe your character, as with seemingly boundless energy you cram more into one day than others do into a week.

THE
HORSE

18

Your Hour of Birth

 WHILE YOUR YEAR OF BIRTH describes your fundamental character, the Animal governing the actual hour in which you were born describes your outer temperament, how people see you or the picture you present to the outside world. Note that each Animal rules over two consecutive hours. Also note that these are GMT standard times and that adjustments need to be made if you were born during Summer or daylight saving time.

11PM – 12.59AM ★ RAT

 Pleasant, sociable, easy to get on with. An active, confident, busy person – and a bit of a busybody to boot.

1AM – 2.59AM ★ OX

 Level-headed and down-to-earth, you come across as knowledgeable and reliable – sometimes, though, a bit biased.

3AM – 4.59AM ★ TIGER

 Enthusiastic and self-assured, people see you as a strong and positive personality – at times a little over-exuberant.

5AM – 6.59AM ★ RABBIT

 You're sensitive and shy and don't project your real self to the world. You feel you have to put on an act to please others.

7AM – 8.59AM ★ DRAGON

 Independent and interesting, you present a picture of someone who is quite out of the ordinary.

9AM – 10.59AM ★ SNAKE

You can be a bit difficult to fathom and, because you appear so controlled, people either take to you instantly, or not at all.

11AM – 12.59PM ★ HORSE

 Open, cheerful and happy-go-lucky is the picture you always put across to others. You're an extrovert and it generally shows.

1PM – 2.59PM ★ SHEEP

 Your unassuming nature won't allow you to foist yourself upon others so people see you as quiet and retiring – but eminently sensible, though.

3PM – 4.59PM ★ MONKEY

 Lively and talkative, that twinkle in your eye will guarantee you make friends wherever you go.

5PM – 6.59PM ★ ROOSTER

 There's something rather stylish in your approach that gives people an impression of elegance and glamour. But you don't suffer fools gladly.

7PM – 8.59PM ★ DOG

 Some people see you as steady and reliable, others as quiet and graceful and others still as dull and unimaginative. It all depends who you're with at the time.

9PM – 10.59PM ★ PIG

 Your laid-back manner conceals a depth of interest and intelligence that doesn't always come through at first glance.

19

Your hour of birth describes your outer temperament.

馬

20

The Horse Lover

Adventurous and independent, there is none more spirited than you, and you have that elusive je ne sais quoi for which Horse-born folk are famous. If you could bottle your sexual fascination, you would be a millionaire. As it is, you're a professional flirt and know just how far to go, how to tease and thrill, how to give all the right signals and come-on cues.

AGILE AND MERCURIAL, you're the Peter Pan of the Chinese Animal signs, perpetually youthful and breezing through life by following your instincts. As well as fervour, yours is the sign of elegance in speech and appearance. Eloquent and persuasive, you can charm the birds from the trees, and very few could match your style. Like the best champagne, you're effervescent and highly intoxicating. Your happiness and enthusiasm fill all those you touch with good cheer and your capacity to live life to the full inspires others to drink deep of the joys of life.

The Horse can seduce the birds from the trees with effortless style.

馬

21

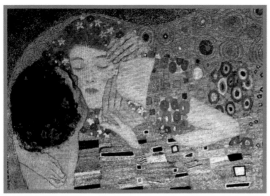

The Kiss
GUSTAV KLIMT 1862–1918

LOVE IS BLIND

As a Horse-born individual, you're a smart cookie in almost every department of life except one – when it comes to love. That's because when you fall in love – which you do all the time – you lose all judgement and throw all reason to the wind. The two aphorisms, 'love is blind' and 'marry in haste, repent at leisure', could have been penned especially for you.

GRAND PASSION

If the truth be told, you fall in love far too quickly and, it would appear, far too often. Each time you fall in love, it's the grand passion. Each time, you throw everything over to follow the object of your desire. This time, this relationship is for keeps, you say; and you say it every time. Ancient Chinese philosophers tell us that when it comes to Horses, maturity brings emotional stability and that's when your relationships are more likely to succeed.

22

In Your Element

ALTHOUGH YOUR SIGN recurs every 12 years, each generation is slightly modified by one of 5 elements. If you were born under the Metal influence your character, emotions and behaviour would show significant variations from an individual born under one of the other elements. Check the Year Chart for your ruling element and discover what effects it has upon you.

THE METAL HORSE ★ 1930 AND 1990

Twice as adventurous, independent and freedom-loving as the average Horse, your fear of being trapped means that you shun commitment. You're a rover, reluctant to put down roots or to settle into a stable relationship. Consequently, you change jobs and partners frequently.

THE WATER HORSE ★ 1942 AND 2002

You're the most indecisive of the equine tribe. Although able to adapt to your circumstances, you tend to be inconsistent and change your mind and direction at the toss of your mane. But you have a sparkling wit and a marvellous sense of humour.

THE WOOD HORSE ★ 1954

The Wood influence helps to temper the Horse's inconsistency and adventurousness, making you less skittish than most. As a consequence, you're able to control excessive restlessness and take a more disciplined approach to life. Ultimately, this brings professional success and stability in your relationships.

THE FIRE HORSE ★ 1906 AND 1966

As a Fire Horse you're a breed apart – volatile and passionate. There's a strong, wild streak in you that makes you want to live on the edge. The Chinese say you leave a trail of devastation behind you wherever you go. Fire Horses fall into two groups: either hugely fortunate and successful or deeply miserable and unlucky.

THE EARTH HORSE ★ 1918 AND 1978

More stable than most other Horses, you work methodically towards a goal. Although in love matters you can be fickle at times, you're not recklessly impulsive and usually weigh up the consequences before you act. Kindness, adaptability and good humour guarantee you easy and happy relationships.

24

*Rencontre
du Soir
(detail)*
THEOPHILE-
ALEXANDRE
STEINLEN
1859–1923

*The Horse
and the Dog
pull in the
same
direction
and could go
far together.*

Partners in Love

THE CHINESE are very definite about which animals are compatible with each other and which are antagonistic. So find out if you're truly suited to your partner.

HORSE + RAT ★
No love lost between you two.

HORSE + OX ★
Better in business together than in bed.

HORSE + TIGER ★
Plenty of high jinks in this high-octane relationship ensure an exciting life together.

HORSE + RABBIT ★
Despite conflicts you could just about put up with each other.

HORSE + DRAGON ★
A powerful chemistry bonds you two sexually.

HORSE + SNAKE ★
Different viewpoints, different agendas spell poor prospects for this union's success.

HORSE + HORSE ★
Two strong-minded, independent individuals suggests little chance of this relationship staying the course.

HORSE + SHEEP ★
Attraction at first sight is followed by galvanic passion and shared desire. This union is for keeps.

Horse with:	Tips on Togetherness	Compatibility
Rat	an unstable union	♥
Ox	confrontational	♥
Tiger	hot and spicy	♥♥♥♥
Rabbit	difficult but achievable	♥♥
Dragon	great sex	♥♥♥
Snake	talking helps to sort it out	♥♥
Horse	terrific passion but, alas, only short-term	♥♥
Sheep	made for each other	♥♥♥♥
Monkey	social yes, sexual no	♥♥
Rooster	quarrels undermine your love	♥♥♥
Dog	you have what it takes	♥♥♥♥
Pig	nice but unrealistic	♥♥

LOVE PARTNERS AT A GLANCE

COMPATIBILITY RATINGS:
♥ *conflict* ♥♥ *work at it* ♥♥♥ *strong sexual attraction* ♥♥♥♥ *heavenly!*

馬
25

HORSE + MONKEY ★
A prickly combination, better for friendship than for marriage.

HORSE + ROOSTER ★
Despite the odd power conflict you make a great team.

HORSE + DOG ★
Tipped for lasting happiness, stability and success.

HORSE + PIG ★
A laid-back sort of affair with lots of indulgent fun, but who would attend to paying the bills or stocking the larder?

Eiaha chipa
PAUL GAUGUIN 1848–1903

Christobel finds Geraldine (detail)
WILLIAM GERSHAM COLLINGWOOD
1854–1932

THE
HORSE

Hot Dates

IF YOU'RE DATING someone for the first time, taking your partner out for a special occasion or simply wanting to re-ignite that flame of passion between you, it helps to understand what would please that person most.

RATS ★ *Wine and dine him or take her to a party. Do something on impulse… go to the races or take a flight in a hot air balloon.*

OXEN ★ *Go for a drive in the country and drop in on a stately home. Visit an art gallery or antique shops. Then have an intimate dinner à deux.*

'So glad to see you…'
COCA-COLA 1945

TIGERS ★ *Tigers thrive on excitement so go clay-pigeon shooting, Formula One racing or challenge each other to a Quasar dual. A date at the theatre will put stars in your Tiger's eyes.*

RABBITS ★ *Gentle and creative, your Rabbit date will enjoy an evening at home with some take-away food and a romantic video. Play some seductive jazz and snuggle up.*

DRAGONS ★ *Mystery and magic will thrill your Dragon date. Take in a son et lumière show or go to a carnival. Or drive to the coast and sink your toes in the sand as the sun sets.*

SNAKES ★ *Don't do anything too active – these creatures like to take life slooooowly. Hire a row-boat for a long, lazy ride down the river. Give a soothing massage, then glide into a sensual jacuzzi together.*

The Carnival
GASTON-DOIN 19/20TH CENTURY

馬

27

HORSES ★ *Your zany Horse gets easily bored. Take her on a mind-spinning tour of the local attractions. Surprise him with tickets to a musical show. Whatever you do, keep them guessing.*

SHEEP ★ *These folk adore the Arts so visit a museum, gallery or poetry recital. Go to a concert, the ballet, or the opera.*

MONKEYS ★ *The fantastical appeals to this partner, so go to a fancy-dress party or a masked ball, a laser light show or a sci-fi movie.*

ROOSTERS ★ *Grand gestures will impress your Rooster. Escort her to a film première or him to a formal engagement. Dressing up will place this date in seventh heaven.*

DOGS ★ *A cosy dinner will please this most unassuming of partners more than any social occasion. Chatting and story telling will ensure a close understanding.*

PIGS ★ *Arrange a slap-up meal or a lively party, or cruise through the shopping mall. Shopping is one of this partner's favourite hobbies!*

馬

28

*Detail from
Chinese
Marriage
Ceremony*
CHINESE
PAINTING

Year of Commitment

CAN THE YEAR in which you marry (or make a firm commitment to live together) have any influence upon your marital relationship or the life you and your partner forge together? According to the Orientals, it certainly can. Whether your marriage is fiery, gentle, productive, passionate, insular or sociable doesn't so much depend on your animal nature, as on the nature of the Animal in whose year you tied the knot.

IF YOU MARRY IN A YEAR OF THE...

RAT ★ *your marriage should succeed because ventures starting now attract long-term success. Materially, you won't want and life is full of friendship.*

Marriage Feast
CHINESE PAINTING

OX ★ *your relationship will be solid and tastes conventional. Diligence will be recognized and you'll be well respected.*

TIGER ★ *you'll need plenty of humour to ride out the storms. Marrying in the Year of the Tiger is not auspicious.*

RABBIT ★ *you're wedded under the emblem of lovers. It's auspicious for a happy, carefree relationship, as neither partner wants to rock the boat.*

DRAGON ★ *you're blessed. This year is highly auspicious for luck, happiness and success.*

SNAKE ★ *it's good for romance but sexual entanglements are rife. Your relationship may seem languid, but passions run deep.*

HORSE ★ *chances are you decided to marry on the spur of the moment as the Horse year encourages impetuous behaviour. Marriage now may be volatile.*

SHEEP ★ *your family and home are blessed but watch domestic spending. Money is very easily frittered away.*

Marriage Ceremony
CHINESE PAINTING

MONKEY ★ *married life could be unconventional. As plans go awry your lives could be full of surprises.*

ROOSTER ★ *drama characterizes your married life. Your household will run like clockwork, but bickering could strain your relationship.*

DOG ★ *it's a truly fortunate year and you can expect domestic joy. Prepare for a large family as the Dog is the sign of fertility!*

PIG ★ *it's highly auspicious and there'll be plenty of fun. Watch out for indulgence and excess.*

馬

29

Marriage Ceremony (detail)
CHINESE PAINTING

Detail from Chinese Marriage Ceremony
CHINESE PAINTING

馬

30

TYPICAL HORSE PLEASURES

COLOUR PREFERENCES ★ *Flame orange*

Topaz

Turquoise

Amethyst

GEMS AND STONES ★ *Amethyst, turquoise, topaz*

SUITABLE GIFTS ★ *Compass, kite, silk shirt, camera, exotic cookbook, embroidery kit, portable phone, pedicure, overnight case, mah-jong set*

HOBBIES AND PASTIMES ★ *Athletics, horse riding, modern dance, theatre, playing wind instruments, flying model aeroplanes*

Church of Saint Anna – Austria

HOLIDAY PREFERENCES ★ *You have itchy feet so travelling is your favourite hobby; the further you can get away the better. An impulsive holiday-maker, you take off on a whim. Sporting or activity holidays suit you best, and camping, trekking and sea voyages are also for you.*

COUNTRIES LINKED WITH THE HORSE ★ *Austria, Romania, Libya, Algeria*

The Horse Parent

STIMULATING YOUR CHILDREN'S imaginations and

encouraging them to think for themselves are the principal tenets that you hold close to your heart. While they're still in their cots, you teach your offspring to value their rights and their freedom. Since Horses buck against restraints, it may be your own drive for freedom that forces your children to stand on their own feet when still comparatively young. Many Horse-born folk make unsentimental parents, who often put their work before, or on a par with, their child-rearing responsibilities.

SPIRIT OF ADVENTURE

In reality, you make an enthusiastic parent whose children grow up with an enquiring mind and an indomitable spirit of adventure – not unlike your own.

31

Young Horses quickly learn how the odds of life are stacked.

THE HORSE HABITAT

There's always a warm welcome at your house since, like all Horses, you make a wonderful host. You like nothing better than spending a convivial evening chatting and dining in company. Evidence of your skill in handicraft will be found in your home, as will be the many projects left in mid-air when something more exciting came along! Golds and oranges, your colours, are used imaginatively to create a vibrant, stimulating environment which is practical as well as comfortable. Housework is not one of your favourite hobbies; in your opinion, life is far too short to spend time dusting the skirting board.

Animal Babies

FOR SOME parents, their children's personalities harmonize perfectly with their own. Others find that no matter how much they may love their offspring they're just not on the same wave-length. Our children arrive with their characters already well formed and, according to Chinese philosophy, shaped by the influence of their Animal Year. So you should be mindful of the year in which you conceive.

BABIES BORN IN THE YEAR OF THE...

RAT ★ *love being cuddled. They keep on the go – so give them plenty of rest. Later they enjoy collecting things.*

OX ★ *are placid, solid and independent. If not left to their own devices they sulk.*

TIGER ★ *are happy and endearing. As children, they have irrepressible energy. Boys are sporty and girls tom-boys.*

RABBIT ★ *are sensitive and strongly bonded to their mother. They need stability to thrive.*

DRAGON ★ *are independent and imaginative from the start. Encourage any interest that will allow their talents to flourish.*

SNAKE ★ *have great charm. They are slow starters so may need help with school work. Teach them to express feelings.*

馬

One Hundred Children Scroll
ANON, MING PERIOD

HORSE ★ *will burble away contentedly for hours. Talking starts early and they excel in languages.*

SHEEP ★ *are placid, well-behaved and respectful. They are family-oriented and never stray too far from home.*

MONKEY ★ *take an insatiable interest in everything. With agile minds they're quick to learn. They're good-humoured but mischievous!*

ROOSTER ★ *are sociable. Bright and vivacious, their strong adventurous streak best shows itself on a sports field.*

DOG ★ *are cute and cuddly. Easily pleased, they are content just pottering around the house amusing themselves for hours. Common sense is their greatest virtue.*

PIG ★ *are affectionate and friendly. Well-balanced, self-confident children, they're happy-go-lucky and laid-back. They are popular with friends.*

馬

34

Horses prefer to live and work on the hoof.

Health, Wealth and Worldly Affairs

TRUE TO YOUR SIGN, when it comes to health you're literally 'strong as a horse'. Your optimistic outlook and positive attitude keep you hale and hearty while your active life-style ensures you get plenty of exercise and fresh air to keep you fighting fit. However, beware the Horse tendency to turn to alcohol and nicotine when under pressure.

Your independent spirit means you like to do things your own way and, if given a free rein, can achieve impressive results, but if your creative expression is stifled, you'll buck like a bronco and head for the hills.

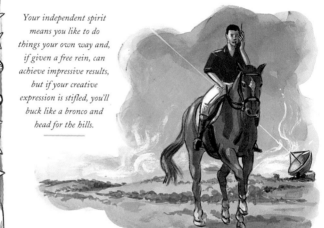

CAREER

With your agile mind, boundless energy, ability to pick up new skills at a glance and willingness to try anything once, you're suited to almost any career you wish to choose. But it's to the world of communications that you're best suited, since you have an inherent talent for languages and a genius for getting through to other people.

FINANCES

As irrepressible in financial matters as in other areas of your life, when it comes to money, you make it and you spend it. Often you'll take risks and gamble, but money brings you huge enjoyment. When you have it, you'll have a good time spending it. When it's gone, you'll go out and make some more.

馬

35

You work best when self-employed although you need a network of contacts. In a creative environment you generate ideas, solve problems and ad-lib, while juggling three or four jobs at the same time. Curbing boredom and learning to work at an even pace would ensure your success.

The Horse is never at a loss in the job market.

FRIENDSHIPS

Though spirited and independent you're also highly gregarious and have a natural herding instinct which compels you to join clubs and associations. You derive immense pleasure in meeting friends for a good chat, and being part of the team is what counts.

HORSES MAKE EXCELLENT:

★ Language teachers ★ Translators ★ Athletes ★
★ Information technologists ★ Librarians ★ Journalists ★
★ Tour operators ★ Pilots ★ Stewards ★ Hoteliers ★
★ Bar-keepers ★ Performers ★ Publicists ★ Show-jumpers ★
★ Holiday-camp entertainers ★ Sales reps ★

East Meets West

COMBINE YOUR Oriental Animal sign with your Western Zodiac birth sign to form a deeper and richer understanding of your character and personality.

ARIES HORSE

★ *Active and enthusiastic, you take life at a gallop. New ideas constantly grab your attention and you tend to leave half-finished projects behind you. Sexually ardent, you don't half come on strong.*

TAUREAN HORSE

★ *Common sense and a practical streak temper your wayward instincts and allow you to take life at a steadier pace. Beware that a tendency to self-centredness doesn't mar your relationships.*

GEMINI HORSE

★ *Clever, persuasive and witty, your charm and good looks mean you are all too often the centre of attention. But you're immature and inconstant in love.*

CANCERIAN HORSE

★ *If you've already found the love of your life all's well. If not, your search for the perfect mate could take time. Once found, he or she will be happy because you have so much love to give.*

LEONINE HORSE

★ *Passionate and strong-willed, once you've made up your mind, nothing will deflect you. This applies to your ambitions as well as to your sexual desires. When you fall in love, you're blind to reason.*

VIRGO HORSE

★ *You're more practical and hard-working than most Horses. Emotionally steadier, you retain your sex appeal whilst keeping both feet on the ground.*

馬

37

LIBRAN HORSE

★ Friends play a very important part in your life. Your charm, light-hearted banter and effervescent personality make you highly in demand at all social occasions. Passionate and sensual, elegant and refined, you do everything in style!

SCORPIO HORSE

★ The Scorpio power of concentration will enable you to focus ideas and see projects through to the end, while the zany outlook of the Horse will lighten Scorpio's emotional intensity. Sexually, this is a potently seductive combination.

SAGITTARIAN HORSE

★ Essentially, this is a union of two Horses, both impulsive and free-wheeling. Coupled together they make you irrepressibly enthusiastic, adventurous and indefatigably optimistic. You love the thrill of the chase so a partner who gives you a good run for your money is a must.

CAPRICORN HORSE

★ You're driven by ambition and a need to succeed. Money and status are important to you and you're prepared to work hard in order to attain the position and standing you aspire to. Faithful and loyal, you're loved and respected by all who know you.

AQUARIAN HORSE

★ You're probably the most colourful of all the Horse-born folk: zany, unconventional and uniquely eccentric. In love, you can be cool and breezy, but you're a caring friend and full of humanitarian zeal.

PISCEAN HORSE

★ Pisces, synonymous with sensitivity, adds gentleness, empathy and a deeply caring instinct to the Horse's brio. With this combination you are a romantic although not slushily sentimental; when you find the partner of your dreams, you give your all to the service of love.

馬

38

FAMOUS HORSES

Lenin

Nelson Mandela

Chopin

Rembrandt

Jimi Hendrix

James Dean

Princess Margaret ★ Paul McCartney ★ Kirk Douglas
Neil Armstrong ★ Clint Eastwood
Chris Evert ★ Billy Graham ★ Degas
Harrison Ford ★ Nelson Mandela
Barbra Streisand ★ Raquel Welch
Catherine Cookson ★ Aretha Franklin
Kevin Costner ★ Tammy Wynette
Billy Wilder ★ Lenin ★ Chopin
Jimi Hendrix ★ Vivaldi
Rita Hayworth ★ James Dean
Rembrandt ★ F D Roosevelt
Leonard Bernstein

Barbra Streisand

The Horse Year in Focus

IN HORSE YEARS there is a sense of hurtling headlong through time. Affairs are spirited, events erratic, trading brisk and emotions volatile. Energy and action characterize the year; acting on impulse and following your instincts will bring success.

GOOD HOUSEKEEPING

Husbandry and good housekeeping are not the most salient of Horse attributes, so keep a tight hold on your purse-strings. The economy will prove unstable; bad management, both personal and political, leads to wild fluctuations in your fortunes, whilst spending and borrowing are likely to go through the roof.

FREE TRAVEL

Freedom is the buzz word, leisure and travel the key. All outdoor pursuits do particularly well under the auspices of the Horse. In this year marriage is on the increase, but so too is divorce.

Horse years encourage you to get up, up and away.

ACTIVITIES ASSOCIATED WITH THE YEAR OF THE HORSE

The discovery, invention, patenting, marketing or manufacturing of: the planet Pluto, perspex, atomic fission, frozen foods, flash bulbs, the structure of DNA, magnetic tape, the theory of the Big Bang.

40

Your Horse Fortunes
for the Next 12 Years

1996 MARKS THE BEGINNING of a new 12-year cycle in the Chinese calendar. How your relationships and worldly prospects fare will depend on the influence of each Animal year in turn.

1996 YEAR OF THE RAT   *19 Feb 1996 – 6 Feb 1997*

As the Rat is your opposite sign this is likely to be a difficult year. Problems and obstacles will dog your steps and slow your progress in almost every area. Romance is unsatisfactory and relationships cause conflict. Keep a low profile.

YEAR TREND: AN UPHILL STRUGGLE

1997 YEAR OF THE OX   *7 Feb 1997 – 27 Jan 1998*

Last year's difficulties have left you champing at the bit, but the Oxen trends still urge caution and you must consolidate your position rather than strike out in new directions. But love brings comfort.

YEAR TREND: CONTINUE TO BIDE YOUR TIME

1998 YEAR OF THE TIGER *28 Jan 1998 – 15 Feb 1999*

At last you get the green light to forge ahead as the vibrant undercurrent to this year is highly conducive to your nature. You'll be partying through 1998 but, while the socializing brings useful contacts, it also cuts deep into your purse.

YEAR TREND: BEWARE FINANCES

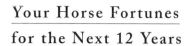

馬

1999 YEAR OF THE RABBIT *16 Feb 1999 – 4 Feb 2000*

If you're seeking a soul mate, romance is likely to be your bugbear this year. New relationships are mismatched or short-lived. Committed Horses fare better and find contentment within the family.

YEAR TREND: **TAKE THINGS EASY**

2000 YEAR OF THE DRAGON *5 Feb 2000 – 23 Jan 2001*

Dragon Years are notoriously unpredictable and give plenty of scope to your inventive genius. Be prepared to grab unexpected opportunities, to travel at the drop of a hat and to cultivate people in high places. In love, temptation is all around you.

YEAR TREND: **STIMULATING**

Under the Dragon, Horses get to make friends and influence people.

2001 YEAR OF THE SNAKE *24 Jan 2001 – 11 Feb 2002*

Clandestine romantic entanglements could well upset the applecart this year with their consequent emotional scenes disturbing your peace of mind. Relationships in general could prove a minefield so be circumspect in all your dealings with others throughout 2001.

YEAR TREND: **BEWARE INTERPERSONAL INVOLVEMENTS**

馬

42

2002 YEAR OF THE HORSE · *12 Feb 2002 – 31 Jan 2003*

Hooray! This is *your* year and you can confidently expand in all areas. New plans will flourish and meet with approval. Follow your instincts but don't upset the status quo in your relationships.

YEAR TREND: A PROSPEROUS YEAR

2003 YEAR OF THE SHEEP · *1 Feb 2003 – 21 Jan 2004*

Stick to the tried and tested at work and put ambitious plans on the back burner. Those of you in the fashion business will find this a prosperous year. Let the Sheep's calming influence help you to cultivate peace and harmony with your loved ones.

YEAR TREND: STEADY PROGRESS

2004 YEAR OF THE MONKEY · *22 Jan 2004 – 8 Feb 2005*

The lively pace of this Monkey year will suit your adventurous nature and you are likely to make great progress. Now's the time to push forward with those ambitious schemes – the more inventive and unusual, the better. True love beckons.

YEAR TREND: KEEP BUSY AND STAY CONFIDENT

In the Rooster's year Horses should slow down to a careful canter.

馬

2005 YEAR OF THE ROOSTER *9 Feb 2005 – 28 Jan 2006*

Though the overall trends for 2005 are progressive, at work you may not achieve as much as you would wish. The secret is to maintain a steady pace and to advance slowly but surely. Social life, friendships and romance make it all worth while.

YEAR TREND: SHORT BREAKS BRING MUCH JOY

2006 YEAR OF THE DOG *29 Jan 2006 – 17 Feb 2007*

An auspicious year when you can make excellent progress. Work, academic studies and sporting activities bring rewards. Stabilizing new relationships, getting married or moving house bring success.

YEAR TREND: OPTIMISM RULES

2007 YEAR OF THE PIG *18 Feb 2007 – 6 Feb 2008*

Money matters come to the forefront this year as finances are positively buoyant; you may even come into a windfall. But what comes in just as easily goes out, as domestic expenses prove a drain on your resources. In love matters, make your feelings known.

YEAR TREND: FINANCIALLY, KEEP ONE STEP AHEAD

PICTURE CREDITS